# Technology All Around Us

# Telecommunications

Anne Rooney

A+
Smart Apple Media

First published in 2005 by Franklin Watts
96 Leonard Street, London EC2A 4XD

Franklin Watts Australia
Level 17/207 Kent Street, Sydney NSW 2000

Produced by Arcturus Publishing Ltd.
26/27 Bickels Yard, 151–153 Bermondsey Street, London SE1 3HA

Series concept: Alex Woolf, Editor: Alex Woolf, Designer: Simon
Borrough, Picture researcher: Glass Onion Pictures

Picture Credits:
Corbis: 24 (Sergei Karpukhin), 25 (Aladin Abdel Naby), 26 (Panasonic
Center/Handout).
Science Photo Library: 4 (Martin Ricdl), 5 (Sheila Terry), 6 (Lawrence
Lawry), 7 (Maximilian Stock Ltd), 8 (Hattie Young), 11, 14 (Mauro
Fermariello), 16 (ESA/CE/Eurocontrol), 17 (Ken M. Johns), 18 (David
Parker), 22 (Tek Image), cover and 28 (Dr. Seth Shostak), 29 (NASA).
Topham Picturepoint: 9 (PA), 10 (Ian Munro), 12, 13, 15 (UPPA), 19
(ImageWorks), 20 (ImageWorks), 21 (Ian Munro), 23, 27 (John Powell).

Published in the United States by Smart Apple Media
2140 Howard Drive West, North Mankato, Minnesota 56003

Library of Congress Cataloging-in-Publication Data

Rooney, Anne.
Telecommunications / by Anne Rooney.
p. cm. — (Technology all around us)
ISBN 1-58340-754-5
1. Telecommunication—Juvenile literature. I. Title. II. Series.

TK5102.4.R66 2005
621.382—dc22                    2004065398

9 8 7 6 5 4 3 2 1

# Contents

Most people today are used to being able to get in touch with friends at the press of a few buttons. We rarely give a thought to the technology that makes this possible, called "telecommunications" systems.

Telecommunications—or telecoms—are a modern development and are still growing and changing rapidly. In a few years, you'll be able to communicate in ways you probably can't imagine now.

## Person to Person

We keep in touch by phone, e-mail, and text messaging, and use the radio, television, and the Internet to find out what's happening in the world. These technologies let us use the written or spoken word—and sometimes pictures or video—to communicate with each other.

Unlike letters, these means of communication are almost immediate, allowing us to hold conversations over long distances.

Using a mobile phone, we can talk to friends wherever we are.

>> **Looking Forward**

### E-mail for the Himalayas

The simputer is a small, handheld device that can be used to send e-mail or voice messages, or to browse the Web. It can be used in any language, as the user writes on the screen with a plastic stylus.

The simputer was launched in 2004. Its developers hope that it will bring telecommunications to people in remote areas of the world, such as the Himalayas.

# Machines Talking

Many electronic devices "talk" to each other, too. Today, you can have a security system in your home that sends a message to your phone if an intruder breaks in, or you can buy a drink from a vending machine using your mobile phone.

Telecommunications are all around us and are becoming more and more important in our lives.

A Morse transmitter used to send telegraphs. The operator uses the large button in the center to tap out the code—a series of short and long signals—which is then sent by wire to a receiving machine. The receiving machine prints out the code as dots and dashes.

## Looking Back

### Telegraph
In 1830, American Joseph Henry sent an electric current along a mile (1.6 km) of wire to ring a bell at the other end. This was the first telegraph and the start of modern telecommunications.

Early telegraph and phone lines were made of metal wire, but newer technologies are often "wireless." Instead of using wires or cables, radio or other signals are sent through the air.

## Cables and Wires

Many telephone networks still use some copper wires, but these are slowly being replaced by new fiber-optic cables.

Optical fibers are strands of glass or plastic, as thin as a human hair, inside a protective coating. They are used in bundles of hundreds or thousands, bound into a cable.

Copper wires carry information as pulses (little bursts) of electrical charge. Fiber-optic cables carry information as light pulses.

Optical fibers, made of glass, carry information coded as pulses of light.

### Looking Forward

**Glass Fiber with No Glass**

In an optical fiber, the light travels down the strand of glass by bouncing off the inside of the coating again and again. Although the glass is very pure, it does slow the light down slightly.

Scientists have developed a new cable that doesn't have glass in the middle—instead, the light is sent through a vacuum, or empty space. There is nothing to slow down the light, and it travels at about 186,400 miles (300,000 km) per second.

### Early Cables

The first communication wires were laid under the sea to carry telegraphs. These quickly failed because they weren't properly protected against water. The first cable between England and France failed after eight days, and the first transatlantic cable lasted only three weeks.

Once cables were laid inside a latex sheath, they worked properly. Later insulators, made of plastic, were even better. The first transatlantic fiber-optic cables were laid in 1988.

Tall towers are used to send out and boost radio signals.

## Airwaves

Wireless communications are sent by radio waves, which travel through the air at the speed of light (see pages 10–11). Radio waves are part of the electromagnetic spectrum, which also includes visible and invisible light, and the microwaves we use for cooking.

A radio signal doesn't need to travel along a particular pathway, like a cable. It is sent into the air, or even into space, and picked up by any receiver tuned to accept it. Radio, television, mobile phones, some remote controls, and wireless computer networks all use radio waves.

7

When you use a phone, the sound of your voice is converted into electrical signals. These travel at the speed of light along the telephone network. If phone calls traveled at the speed of sound, there would be a long gap between one person speaking and the other hearing it.

## There's Nobody There...

Many businesses no longer have lots of people communicating by phone—they use computers instead. You might "talk" to a computer if you buy theater tickets over the phone or need advice on fixing a product. Instead of speaking to a person, you will be asked to make choices by pressing numbers on your phone.

A cordless phone can be carried around the house and used anywhere that is comfortable or convenient.

People who work in call centers deal with phoned-in questions or orders all day. Because phones offer instant communication around the world, many call centers are being moved to places such as India, where wages and housing costs are lower.

## Looking Forward

**Voice recognition**

Scientists are working on "voice recognition" computer systems that can understand speech and answer phone calls. This is very difficult to accomplish. The computer needs to be able to distinguish between words that sound similar, and to ignore extra noises like "um" and "er." It must also deal with different accents and people who speak quickly or slowly.

## Not Just Voice

The phone network isn't used only for voice calls. It's also used to send fax messages.

Fax machines send an image of a piece of paper from one place to another. The sender's fax machine scans the paper, making a picture of it coded as a set of electrical pulses. The receiving fax machine changes these electrical pulses back to an image and prints it out on paper.

## Looking Back

### Telex

Before the fax machine was invented, there were two ways of getting a written message from one place to another using phone lines: telegraph or telex. Telegraphs went through a main telegraph office to be converted from dots and dashes back to words, but telex could be sent directly from person to person.

Telex stands for "*tele*printer *ex*change." The message is typed into a telex machine, which is like a mechanical typewriter. It is automatically typed out on another telex machine at the receiving end.

Radio can be transmitted through the air or through space. It can even pass through buildings and other solid objects. Most wireless communications use radio, although a few use infrared waves.

## Radio Waves

Radio is transmitted as "waves" of energy. Radio waves can carry sound, pictures, or computer data. They are sent out by a radio transmitter.

A radio signal is decoded by a radio receiver, which might be a mobile phone, TV, radio, or part of a computer network. The receiver changes the variations in the radio wave back into sound or data.

## Digital Radio

Most radio transmitters can send a radio signal only 31 to 37 miles (50–60 km) over land before it breaks up. National radio stations use extra transmitters around the country to boost the signal.

New satellite radio transmitters broadcast digital radio (see pages 16–17). The signal arrives from 21,750 miles (35,000 km) above Earth and is much clearer.

The voice of the disk jockey in this radio studio is broadcast as waves sent out by a radio transmitter. The waves are picked up by radio receivers in people's homes and cars.

You can also listen to radio stations on your computer to get a clear signal. You can play the sound using the radio station's Web page and your computer's sound system. The sound is carried as data over the Internet, just like pictures and text.

Technology in Action

### Marconi and the First Radio

The concept of radio was introduced in 1860, but it did not become reality until the 1890s. Two men worked separately on radio, and both claimed to have invented it: Italian inventor Guglielmo Marconi and Croatian Nikola Tesla, working in the United States.

Marconi sent the first signal across the English Channel in 1899 and the first signal across the Atlantic two years later. The message was Morse code for the letter "S."

Guglielmo Marconi with his radio equipment. In 1909, he won a Nobel Prize for physics for his work in radio communication.

### Radio School

The Alice Springs School of the Air has 140 students, but they live in an area of 385,000 square miles (1,000,000 sq km) in the Australian outback. They are too far away from each other to attend a school building.

Instead, they use the Internet and two-way radio to share lessons with other children and teachers. The school broadcasts a message to students each morning. Children have three class lessons a week, as well as one individual 10-minute lesson.

Mobile telephones help us keep in touch with others wherever we are. Because they communicate with the phone network by radio, they don't need any wires or cables.

# Mobile Phones

A man herding horses in the mountains of Chile uses a mobile phone to communicate with other herders.

## Cells and Bases

Mobile phones are often referred to as "cell phones" because the phone networks break each country into "cells," or small areas. Each cell has a base station that handles all of the calls and messages for each phone in its area. From the base station, a call is passed to the rest of the phone network or sent out to the phone that needs it.

To make or receive calls, a phone must be suitably close to a base station. This works well in most places, but in remote areas, mobile phones sometimes don't work. And inside large buildings or underground, there is often too much solid material for the radio waves to transmit properly.

## Looking Forward

**Dial-a-drink**

We will soon be able to pay by mobile phone for parking, snacks, and other cheap items. The Swedish telephone company Nokia has developed a system that lets a person press number buttons on the phone to order a drink from a vending machine. The cost of the item is charged to the phone bill.

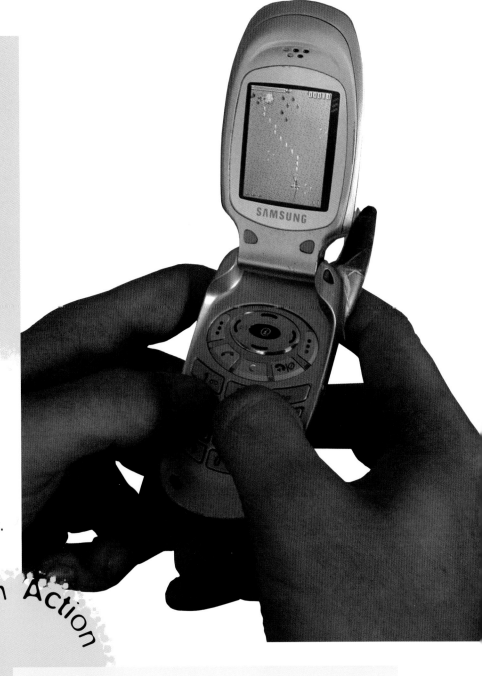

Many young people like to play games on their cell phones.

In some places, such as hospitals and airplanes, cell phones aren't allowed because the radio signals might interfere with other equipment.

## Fun and Games

The latest mobile phones have extra functions, such as games, built-in cameras, or radios. Some have multi-player games to play with other phone users.

The most advanced phones, called third-generation (3G) phones, can even receive short video clips. In Britain, one television channel sends news bulletins that can be watched on 3G phones.

Technology in Action

**Phone Music**

Many people like to buy or compose new ring tones for their phones. In 2004, the German pop group Panda Babies became the first band to release an album using only polyphonic ring tones, with no CD available.

Polyphonic ring tones have high-quality sound nearly as good as a CD. The Panda Babies album must be downloaded from the Internet and can be played only on a phone.

Many people enjoy playing multi-player games on their phones or sending text messages to each other.

When mobile phones were first developed, phone companies added a way of sending text messages to help phone engineers set up and test networks. But text messaging became so popular with customers that it's now the most common use of mobile phones in some countries.

## TXT 4 U

On early phones, users had to press a number key several times to get a single letter. Because it took so long to key in a message, and because messages could be only 163 characters long, people developed a special "txt msg" shorthand language.

New phones use a system called "predictive text input." With this, a number key is pressed only once for each letter, and the phone guesses which word you want. Many newer phones also allow longer messages, automatically breaking them into a series of linked short messages.

Flight Information
Arriving at the airport only to find that your plane's delayed could soon be a thing of the past. On August 1, 2003, the two airports in Rome—Ciampino and Fiumicino—introduced a text message update service for people meeting or taking flights. For a small fee, messages giving up-to-date flight information are sent.

# PIX 4 U

Many cell phones have digital cameras so users can take a picture to send as a message or store on a computer. It's also possible to send pictures downloaded from a Web site.

The Web site of the National Gallery in London sells images of pictures in its collections, which can be sent directly to your cell phone.

This man is using his phone to take a photo of the religious festival Rathayatra.

## Looking Back

**Pager Language**
Before text messaging, many American teenagers used pagers to keep in touch with each other. Pagers are small electronic devices that can receive a short message in text or often just in numbers.

The codes teenagers used were based on the way some letters look like numbers. For example: 90*401773 means GO HOME.

This is because "9" looks like "g"; "0" = "O"; "4" looks like "h" upside down; "177" looks a little like "m"; and "3" looks like "E" backward.

A satellite is something that orbits Earth or another planet. The moon is Earth's only natural satellite. Modern communications use artificial satellites to broadcast signals across Earth.

Each of these Inmarsat-3 satellites covers part of Earth's surface with its transmissions. Between them, they cover the entire planet.

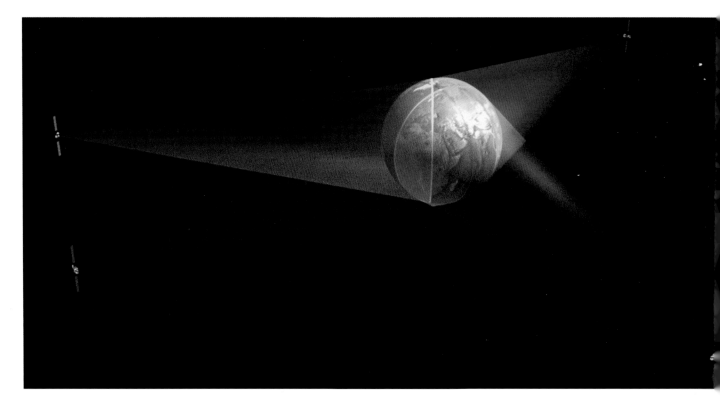

## Our Presence in Space

Satellites are launched into space on the back of a rocket or aboard a space shuttle. There are currently about 26,000 satellites in orbit, including working satellites, old satellites no longer in use, and various bits of "space junk."

## How We Use Satellites

Satellites have many uses. We use them to transmit phone, radio, or TV signals. Others are used for navigation or to locate specific positions on Earth. Some pick up distress signals broadcast in emergencies, letting rescuers know where help is needed so they can get there quickly.

## Looking Back

*Sputnik*

The first artificial satellite was *Sputnik 1*, launched by the Soviet Union in 1957. It worked for only three weeks before its battery ran out. During this time, it sent radio signals to Earth. These signals reported temperature changes measured by instruments on *Sputnik 1*. The tone of a "beep" varied to show the change in temperature. *Sputnik 1* burned up in Earth's atmosphere after 92 days.

Satellites are also used for spying, military operations, monitoring climate change, and looking into space.

# Where are You?

Global positioning systems (GPS) help us locate people or vehicles carrying special GPS devices. The position of a GPS device can be pinpointed exactly using information collected from satellites.

Some mobile phones contain GPS devices. GPS is also used by shipping companies and the police for tracking vehicles, and by explorers, soldiers, and others who go into dangerous areas from which they might need to be rescued.

Technology in Action

**Where in the World?**
**In January 2004, 14 fishermen were stranded on a lump of ice that broke free in Lake Erie. They called for help using cell phones but could not say where they were. Luckily, the fishermen had GPS receivers, so rescue personnel could get to them using satellite information.**

This field geologist can check his location using a handheld GPS receiver. He is able to pinpoint where he is to within 330 feet (100 m).

We all use television without a second thought for news, education, entertainment—and even to receive information we don't really want, such as advertisements for products.

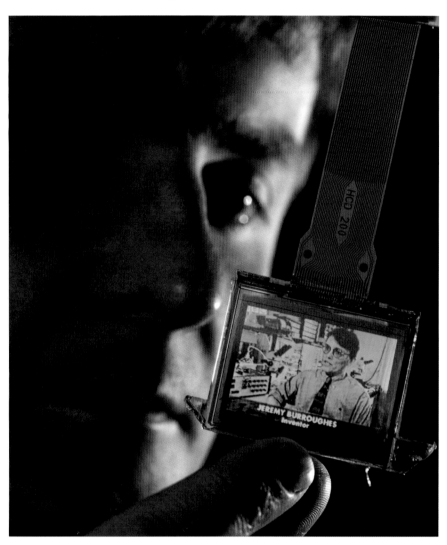

An ultra-thin plastic **TV** screen about 1/10th-inch (2 mm) thick— the portable **TV** of the future?

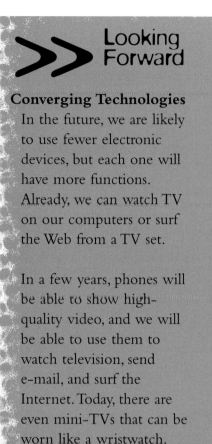

>> Looking Forward

**Converging Technologies**
In the future, we are likely to use fewer electronic devices, but each one will have more functions. Already, we can watch TV on our computers or surf the Web from a TV set.

In a few years, phones will be able to show high-quality video, and we will be able to use them to watch television, send e-mail, and surf the Internet. Today, there are even mini-TVs that can be worn like a wristwatch.

## How it Works

Television signals, like radio signals, were originally sent through the air and picked up by an antenna at each home that had a television. Television antennas are gradually disappearing as more and more people subscribe to cable or satellite television.

Cable TV is transmitted through underground fiber-optic cables. To keep people from watching the channels for free, cable companies send the signals in code. Viewers need a special box to decode the channels.

Satellite TV is broadcast over a wide area by communications satellites. To receive satellite signals, you need a satellite dish that is positioned to face the satellite that broadcasts the channels you want.

Technology in Action

Journalists working in the desert in Kuwait use technology linked by satellite to send video reports to London.

## Digital TV

Digital TV uses a different method of sending TV signals. It sends them in the form of separate tiny pulses rather than in continuous radio waves, which are called "analog signals." Digital signals produce a much sharper image than analog TV.

Eventually, broadcasters will stop sending out analog signals and replace them all with digital TV signals.

### Embedded Journalists

The war in Iraq in 2003 saw journalists for TV stations, radio stations, and newspapers working alongside (or "embedded with") allied troops to report on the war.

Instead of sending their reports from a safe distance behind the action, many journalists used advanced communications technology to make and send their reports from the front line. Reports were transmitted by satellite and often broadcast live around the world.

The Internet is the worldwide network of computers that is used for sharing and communicating information. Most people use the Internet for e-mail and the World Wide Web.

## Changing the World

Anyone can publish Web pages, which means we can share interests and problems with people around the world and find information on any topic in just seconds.

But the Web means much more to people in some countries. It has changed the way we find out news and has made it much harder to keep secrets. Although some countries try to restrict Internet access, it's difficult to block it completely.

Web logs, or "blogs," are a kind of online diary. Web logs kept by U.S. soldiers in Iraq in 2003 gave an account of everyday life in a war while it was happening in a way that was not possible before.

In a **cybercafe**, a customer can use the Internet to browse the Web or send e-mail.

## Moving Life Online

More and more of our daily activities can be carried out over the Internet. We can shop, manage our finances, book tickets for travel and events, play games, and communicate instantly with distant friends. We can even diagnose illnesses without visiting a doctor. Soon we may even be able to vote in elections online.

With a credit card, it's easy to shop online, ordering tickets or goods from a Web page.

## Looking Back

### Predicting the World Wide Web

The World Wide Web started in 1990, but in 1945, American Vannevar Bush suggested building a computer system that would show people linked pages of information and pictures. His idea was far ahead of its time, although his system looked nothing like the computers we use for Web browsing today.

## Looking Forward

### The Interplanetary Internet

Soon the World Wide Web may not be restricted to this world. Plans are being made to put computers on other planets in our solar system. They would communicate by radio at first, but eventually they would use laser light.

The first step is likely to place a set of relay satellites around Mars that could be used by spacecraft to communicate with Earth. Work may start in 2005, but a full interplanetary network won't be in place before 2040.

# Talking Online

"Chat" used to mean just speaking. Now we can "chat" online by typing a conversation. This can be a private chat between friends who have agreed to talk to each other, or a discussion in a public chat room where anyone can join in.

Each person typcs messages from his or her own computer; the messages are shown on the computers of everyone else taking part in the chat.

## Who Are You Talking To?

We can chat online to communicate with people we already know or use a chat room to meet people who share a particular interest. Online celebrity chat rooms give people the chance to ask questions to famous writers, singers, actors, or politicians.

Chatting can be just for fun, or it can be a way of exchanging serious information. For example, Internet support groups for people with rare medical problems bring together sufferers from around the world so that they can share experiences and solutions to problems.

## Looking Back

### Bulletin Boards

Before online chatting and Web logs, one way in which people shared news and information on the Internet was by using online bulletin boards. Anyone can "post" a message, and everyone else can read it.

In 1991, during the final months of the Communist regime in the Soviet Union, many Russians posted information on Internet bulletin boards or sent e-mails to friends and family in other countries, giving them valuable information about what was happening.

Chatting online is a good way of keeping in touch with distant friends and relatives. It's cheaper than a long-distance phone call and quicker than a letter.

# Safe Chatting

On the Internet, people can easily pretend to be someone they're not. It is important that kids use caution in chat rooms and notify parents or teachers if something offensive or dangerous is said. It's safest to chat only with people you already know well.

This wireless computer for children can be used to send e-mail, chat, play games, and surf the Web.

 Looking Forward

### Smile!

New developments could make online chatting more of a face-to-face experience. One plan involves taking a digital photo of a person's face and reducing it to the most important parts: the eyes, lips, nose, and eyebrows.

Such a small image could be transmitted over the Internet quickly enough to work as a real-time, moving face, showing emotions during an online chat.

We can use telecom technologies to help us see what's happening in places we can't get to. For many of us, that might mean looking at a Web page to see a picture sent from a special place or event.

This man, in a cybercafe in Moscow, Russia, is watching a live Webcast of an interview with Russian president Vladimir Putin.

## Webcams and Webcasts

A Webcam is a digital camera linked to a Web page so that it shows an up-to-date picture of a particular place. For example, when a panda in the San Diego Zoo had a baby in August 2003, the zoo set up a Webcam so that people around the world could watch the baby grow. The panda cam was so popular that other zoos followed its example.

A Webcast is a broadcast, like a TV program, on the World Wide Web. To watch the Webcast, you just need to open the right Web page. Webcasts of sporting events, carnivals, and rock concerts mean that people who can't attend can still enjoy the event.

## Keeping an Eye on Things

Pictures sent from remote cameras can be used for spying and surveillance. The pictures can be sent over the Internet, like a Webcast or Webcam, or they can be sent by radio to a receiver.

## Looking Forward

### Roboroach and Roborat

Scientists are using implants to make remote-controlled "cockroaches" and "rats" that can be steered into buildings or disaster sites.

The robotic cockroaches, the work of a team in Japan, will carry tiny cameras and microphones in a "backpack." They can be used for spying or to help locate people trapped in rubble after an earthquake or explosion.

The "rats," created in New York, are controlled by electronic impulses and serve many of the same functions as the cockroaches.

Experts in California test the *Pyramid Rover.* The robot was sent to explore an air shaft in the Queen's Chamber of Egypt's Great Pyramid.

**Technology in Action**

### Exploring the Mystery of the Great Pyramid
On September 18, 2002, archaeologists sent a remote-controlled robot into a mysterious tunnel in an Egyptian pyramid. The tunnel ended in a sealed door.

Following radioed instructions, the robot drilled a hole in the door and poked through a fiber-optic camera to look into the room for the first time in 4,500 years. They found only another door, so archeologists will have to do further work to discover the pyramid's secrets.

In the future, we may not need to be home to control what happens in our houses. It will be possible to turn equipment on and off remotely.

This kitchen table with a touch-screen surface is part of a display of how our homes may look after 2010. People can access the Internet by touching the table.

## Phone Home

Some appliances in our homes will soon be controlled by mobile phone. You will be able to turn up the heat before getting home if the weather gets colder, set the DVD recorder, or preheat the oven.

If someone comes to the door while you're out, you'll be able to see and talk to him or her from a Web page linked to a security system. Some new houses in Australia are already being built with these capabilities.

## Talking Refrigerators

Scientists are working on household appliances that can "talk" to each other without people around. They are developing refrigerators that can check what food is left in them and order more over the Internet. To let the fridge "know" what it contains, the owner will need to scan the bar code on the food put in and taken out.

### Home Help
People with disabilities are being helped at home by remote-controlled and wireless equipment. In a specially equipped home, radio and infrared remote controls can be used to open and close windows or curtains, operate doors and locks, adjust the heating, and control music or TV channels in all rooms.

Houses can also have special alarm systems installed that can detect if the person living there has had an accident and call for help.

*We use remote controls for TVs and stereos. Soon, we'll be using them to control other equipment in our homes.*

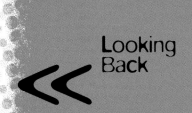

## Looking Back

### Remote Control TVs
Remote control was used by the German military to control speed boats in World War I. It was first used in homes to open garage doors in the 1940s.

The first wireless TV remote control, developed in 1955, was operated by a flashlight. The light was detected by sensors on the screen. Unfortunately, this meant that bright sunlight on the screen could change channels.

The first TV remote to use ultrasound (very high-pitched sound that we can't hear) was designed in 1956. In the 1980s, infrared replaced ultrasound.

As we explore farther and farther into space, we will need to invent new ways of communicating to keep in touch with spacecraft millions of miles away.

## Radio from Space

Radio telescopes pick up radio signals from deep space. We use these signals to learn about the history of the universe and the composition of distant stars. We also send our own signals into space in hopes of getting a reply from intelligent beings elsewhere in the universe.

The Parkes radio telescope in New South Wales, Australia. Its dish is 210 feet (64 m) across and is used to pick up radio waves from space.

 Looking Forward

**Sending Secrets through Space**

Even though we can't yet reach distant stars, scientists are exploring ways of keeping messages safe when they send them between galaxies. One suggestion is that a message could be split into two beams of photons (tiny particles of light) and bounced off mirrors in space, coming back together only at the destination.

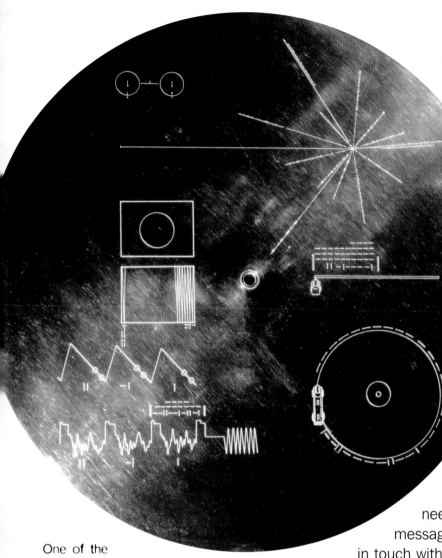

# Keeping in Touch in Space

Even though radio waves travel at the speed of light, distances in space are so vast that it can take years for a radio signal from deep space to reach Earth.

The distance traveled by light in one year is called a light-year. The closest star to our sun is 4.3 light-years away—this means a radio signal would take more than four years to get from the star to Earth! Even a signal from the outer limits of our solar system would take 10 hours.

If we traveled far into space, we would need to find faster means of sending messages, so that the spacecraft could keep in touch with Earth.

One of the Golden Records— the gold disks carried by the *Voyager 1* spacecraft that has been sent into space with messages for any beings that may find it.

## Looking Back

### Hello, Universe

In 1977, the spacecraft *Voyager 1* was sent to explore distant space. Signals to control it now take more than 12 hours to reach the craft and are very weak when they arrive.

*Voyager 1* is nearing the edge of our solar system. It carries messages for any alien spacecraft it may meet. These include sounds, words, and pictures stored on gold disks, as well as greetings in 54 languages and a map of Earth's location in the universe.

# Timeline

| | |
|---|---|
| **1200 B.C.E.** | The ancient Greeks use fires to send signals over long distances. |
| **37 B.C.E.** | The Romans use a "heliograph," a system of mirrors to send messages with flashes of sunlight. |
| **A.D. 1793** | The first commercial semaphore system is set up in France. Two movable mechanical arms on a pole are used to signal letters of the alphabet, according to their positions. |
| **1830** | Joseph Henry rings a bell a mile (1.6 km) away by sending an electrical signal along a wire. |
| **1838** | The first commercial telegraph line is built between Washington and Baltimore. |
| **1876** | Alexander Graham Bell patents the telephone. |
| **1878** | The first telephone exchange opens in New Haven, Connecticut. |
| **1895** | Radio is invented. |
| **1920** | The first public radio broadcasts, started by Guglielmo Marconi in Britain. |
| **1936** | The first public TV broadcasts begin in Britain, created by the BBC. |
| **1953** | Color television is developed in the U.S. |
| **1957** | The first artificial satellite, *Sputnik 1*, is launched by the Soviet Union. |
| **1962** | The first communications satellite goes into service. |
| **1966** | Optical fibers are developed. |
| **1969** | ARPANET, linking the computers of four universities together and forming the basis of the Internet, is formed; e-mail first used on ARPANET. |
| **1978** | The first GPS system is developed by the U.S. Air Force. |
| **1979** | The first mobile phone is developed in the U.S. |
| **1983** | The Internet evolves from ARPANET; mobile phones become available to the public. |
| **1990** | The World Wide Web is founded by British physicist Tim Berners-Lee. |
| **1993** | The first Web browser that can show text and pictures together is developed. |
| **1997** | The development of WAP (wireless application protocol) means that mobile phones can be used to browse the Web. |

# Glossary

**analog** Information in the form of a continuous stream or wave.

**antenna** A wire or metal rod used to transmit or receive radio or television signals.

**archaeologist** A person who studies the past by finding and examining old objects and buildings.

**base station** A station that provides a communications service for all the mobile phones in an area and forms their link to the larger phone network.

**broadcast** Send out a television or radio program.

**cell** An area defined for the operation of mobile (cell) phones, which is served by a base station.

**character** A letter, number, or punctuation mark.

**data** Information, or the raw facts and figures that can be turned into meaningful information.

**digital** Information in the form of pulses.

**digital photo** A photograph that is recorded digitally on a computer rather than on photographic film.

**electromagnetic spectrum** The range of energy that exists as waves, including visible and invisible light, X rays, and radio waves.

**fiber-optic cable** Cable made of bunches of optical fibers—thin, glass fibers used to carry data as pulses of light.

**implant** Something artificial that is put into the body of a person or animal.

**infrared** Energy in the form of light that is invisible to people but can be felt as heat and (with special goggles) used to show things in the dark. Infrared can be used for remote control over a short distance, but it can't go around corners or through solid objects.

**insulators** Materials that can't carry electricity (or heat). Insulators are used around cables that carry electricity to keep the electricity in the cable.

**latex** A material made of rubber or artificial rubber.

**network** A set of computers, phones, or other equipment linked together to communicate and share information.

**online** Connected to the Internet.

**pulse** A small burst of activity or energy, often of electricity or light.

**receiver** A piece of equipment set up to accept signals (such as radio or television signals).

**satellite** A natural or artificial object that orbits a planet.

**scan** Make an image from something.

**Soviet Union** Also known as the USSR (Union of Soviet Socialist Republics), a country formed from the territories of the Russian Empire in 1917, which lasted until 1991.

**space junk** Items left in space that are no longer used or needed.

**stylus** A small, plastic stick that looks like a pen and is used to point to things on, or write on, a touch-sensitive screen.

**surveillance** Watching someone or something, usually secretly.

**transatlantic** Crossing the Atlantic ocean.

**transmitter** A piece of equipment used to send out radio waves so that they can be picked up at a distant location.

**tuned** Set to pick up and make sense of a particular source or type of radio wave.

**typewriter** A mechanical or electric machine for producing text. It works by pressing a metal key with a single character against a ribbon treated with ink so that it presses onto a piece of paper and makes a mark in the shape of the character.

# Further Information

## Further Reading

Maddison, Simon. *Telecommunications*. London: Franklin Watts, 2003.

Masters, Anthony. *Pictures Through the Air: The Story of John Logie Baird*. London: Hodder Wayland, 2001.

Parker, Steve. *1960s: The Satellite Age*. Milwaukee, Wis.: Heinemann Library, 2002.

Rooney, Anne. *Internet Technologies*. North Mankato, Minn.: Chrysalis, 2003.

## Web sites

**http://www.howstuffworks.com**
A site that explains how many types of telecommunications equipment work.

**http://voyager.jpl.nasa.gov**
Find out about how we communicate with spacecraft sent from Earth.

**http://www.pbs.org/wgbh/aso/thenandnow/tech.html**
Discover how inventors and inventions helped shape the modern world.